I0815357

Historical Disasters

Titanic

by Julie Murray

Dash!
LEVELED READERS
An Imprint of Abdo Zoom • abdobooks.com

Level 1 – Beginning
Short and simple sentences with familiar words or patterns for children who are beginning to understand how letters and sounds go together.

Level 2 – Emerging
Longer words and sentences with more complex language patterns for readers who are practicing common words and letter sounds.

Level 3 – Transitional
More developed language and vocabulary for readers who are becoming more independent.

abdobooks.com

Published by Abdo Zoom, a division of ABDO, PO Box 398166, Minneapolis, Minnesota 55439.

Printed in the United States of America, North Mankato, Minnesota.
052023
092023

Photo Credits: Alamy, Getty Images, Granger Collection, Shutterstock
Production Contributors: Kenny Abdo, Jennie Forsberg, Grace Hansen, John Hansen
Design Contributors: Candice Keimig, Neil Klinepier

Library of Congress Control Number: 2022947149

Publisher's Cataloging in Publication Data

Names: Murray, Julie, author.
Title: Titanic / by Julie Murray
Description: Minneapolis, Minnesota : Abdo Zoom, 2024 | Series: Historical disasters | Includes online resources and index.
Identifiers: ISBN 9781098281267 (lib. bdg.) | ISBN 9781098281960 (ebook) | ISBN 9781098282318 (Read-to-me ebook)
Subjects: LCSH: Disasters--Juvenile literature. | History--Juvenile literature. | Titanic (Steamship)-Juvenile literature.
Classification: DDC 910.91--dc23

Table of Contents

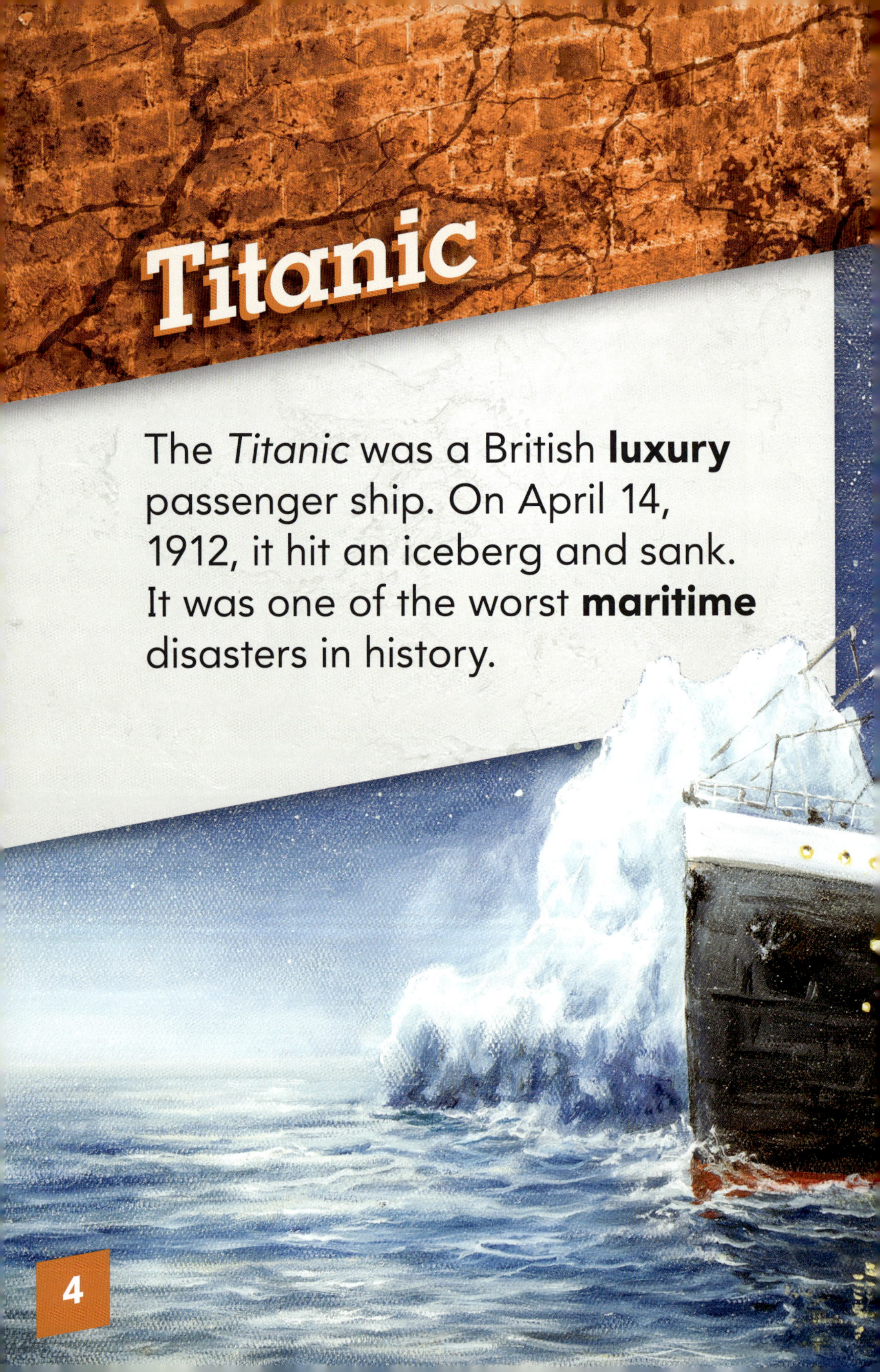

Titanic

The *Titanic* was a British **luxury** passenger ship. On April 14, 1912, it hit an iceberg and sank. It was one of the worst **maritime** disasters in history.

Maiden Cruise

Construction of the *Titanic* began on March 31, 1909. The ship took three years to build. At the time, it was the largest ship in the world.

It set sail on its **maiden cruise** from Southampton, England, on April 10, 1912. The 2,240 people on board, including passengers and crew, were headed for New York.

Four days into the trip across the Atlantic Ocean disaster struck!

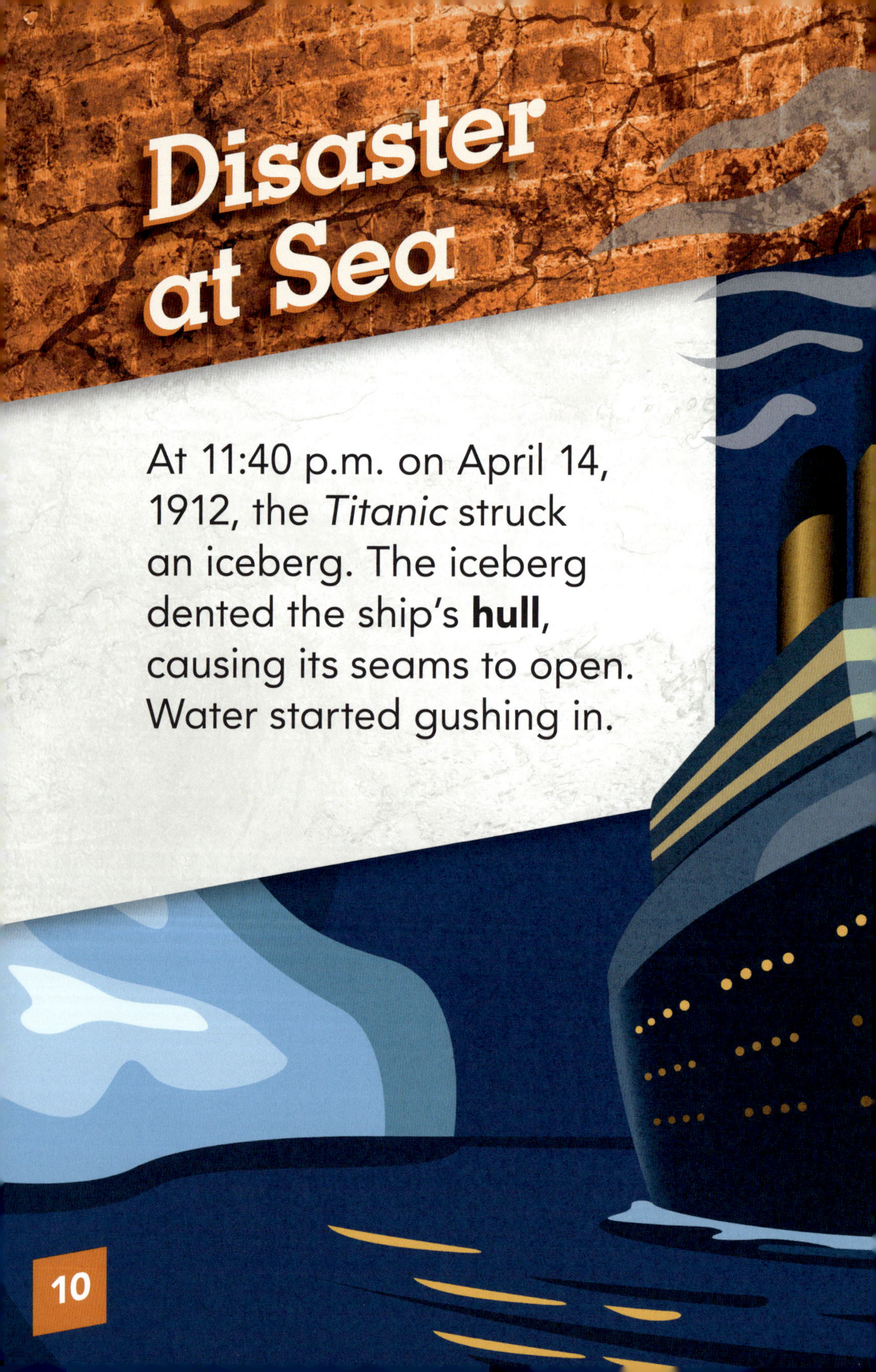

Disaster at Sea

At 11:40 p.m. on April 14, 1912, the *Titanic* struck an iceberg. The iceberg dented the ship's **hull**, causing its seams to open. Water started gushing in.

The ship's alarms went off. Passengers put on life jackets and many headed to the lifeboats. There were only enough lifeboats to carry half of the passengers on board. This was because the ship was said to be unsinkable.

Some passengers panicked and jumped overboard. The water was a frigid 28° F (-2° C). Many people in the water died from **hypothermia**.

At 2:20 a.m. on April 15, 1912, the *Titanic* sank to the bottom of the ocean.

Many went down with the ship including the *Titanic's* captain, Edward John Smith.

TITANIC
DISASTER
GREAT LOSS
OF LIFE
EVENING NEWS

More than 1,500 people lost their lives in the disaster. Only 340 bodies were recovered. The rest were lost at sea.

The wreckage was found in 1985. The *Titanic* rested on the ocean floor 12,500 feet (3,810 m) below the surface.

More than 6,000 **artifacts** have been recovered. They can be seen at exhibits around the world.

More Facts

- The *Titanic* was a giant ship. It was 883 feet long (269 m). That is almost as long as three football fields!
- The ship's full name was *RMS Titanic*. RMS stands for Royal Mail Steamer. The ship was carrying 3,500 sacks of letters and packages.
- The blockbuster movie *Titanic* came out in 1997. It won 11 Academy Awards, including Best Picture.

Glossary

artifact – any object made by human beings, especially one of an earlier era.

hull – the rigid frame or outer shell of a ship.

hypothermia – a condition of very low body temperature.

luxury – something very pleasant but not necessary.

maiden cruise – the first voyage of a ship.

maritime – of or relating to sea ships or navigation of the sea.

Index

Online Resources

To learn more about the *Titanic*, please visit **abdobooklinks.com** or scan this QR code. These links are routinely monitored and updated to provide the most current information available.